PAINTED BUTTERFLY

A POETRY COLLECTION

Copyright © 2019 Amaka Oguejiofo.
All rights reserved. First paperback edition printed 2019 in the United Kingdom a
catalogue record for this book is available
from the British Library.
ISBN 978-0-9934611-2-5
No part of this book shall be reproduced or transmitted in any form or by
any means, electronic or mechanical, including photocopying, recording, or by any information retrieval system without written permission of the publisher.
Published by Scribblecity Publications.
Printed in Great Britain
Although every precaution has been taken in
the preparation of this book, the publisher and author assume no responsibility for errors or omissions. Neither is any liability assumed for damages resulting from the use of this information
contained herein.

FOREWORD

This creative writing exercise, by the author of *Painted Butterfly: A Poetry Collection*, Amaka Oguejiofo, is both audacious and ambitious because for a first collection of poems, it is not only a bold move, but it captures the minds of the reading audience. This is a most worthy literary venture in a clime where female poets are in want and there is no better way to launch out as a poet than with much colours and gait. The most visible attribute of a butterfly is its possession of beautifully coloured wings in all shades and hues, bright or dim. Therefore, the choice of title for this collection of poems, Painted Butterfly, is very significant as it suggests ahead of reading, the eclectic nature of the collection and its preoccupation with nature.

This book is a collection of 77 poems altogether, spread across a variety of themes, plots and settings. It is equally instructive that the first of the 77 poems in the collection is titled "Colours" in harmonious relationship with the book title, *Painted Butterfly*. In the poem, "Colours", Amaka Oguejiofo sets the overall mood of the subsequent poems which follow. The poet persona is an artist who pleads to paint another persona in all colours. The writer's attempt at directing the readers' attention to the visual representation of colours may seem, to the non-literary mind, like addressing nothing, yet she, in that gaiety of mood, addresses everything as a potential source of joy. Here is a way to make humans see all things with sunny disposition; the implication being, if they are colourful, then they can also be inspirational.

"Woman 1" is a fascinating reading experience for a reader. Without being controversial or confrontational, the poem presents the strength of a woman, but it also lists a number of responsibilities and burdens, both biologically acquired and socially inherited. She does not judge, she only makes the reader understand the enormity of these responsibilities. The strength of this poem also lies in the ability of the poet to trust her reading audience to form positive opinions in the elaborate exposition she has made. However, running through the poems, the influences of the poet's belief system cannot be overlooked in her subtle demand for introspection and deep reflection as revealed in the poems; "Prayer" and "Inspiration." "At the Ocean's Edge" is a beautiful description of nature even by its carefully chosen title, it tells of nature's beauty but it also tells of its mystical expressions of self. The last line, "I am bigger" is a subtle reference to a maker of beauty who also makes man dominate the works of His hands. In the same way, "Jigsaw Puzzle" and "Dark Nights" combine all of these elements with the theme of internal conflict and the constant loss of virtues in emerging African societies.

The overall mood of the poetry collection gives off an impression of the poet as a pacifist or die-hard optimist, because of the poet's deliberate effort to inject colours, laughter and inspirational messages in the body of the poems. It is therefore, a pleasant reading experience to be confronted with the shock of bloody and violent images in "Blood on the Plateau." This clearly marks a difference from the overall mood of this collection of poems, the writer, at this point becomes implicated in the sociopolitical realities of her environment and therefore, takes a further step out of her comfort zone, to play the role of a mouthpiece for a suffering nation. This simple act defines her relationship with a troubled society. More instructive is the myriad of rhetorical questions raised to indict the nation's leadership in the bloodletting and life wastages caused by poor leadership – "Where are the Lords of the land? The ancient warriors? Where are the owners of the land? / Asleep? Do they lie supine when death walks the land rattling its bones in its wake?" The pain of a nations' tragedy are clearly expressed in these questions, and by raising questions, she calls for solutions to a national tragedy.

"The Return" and "We Were like You" are nostalgic recollections of the remote past, but while the former is nostalgic about African communal lifestyle, the latter presents antithetical relationship between dwellers of the past and that of the present; the youth and the aged, modernity and the traditional. It becomes more interesting when the poet concludes that "…someday, you will be like us." Here is an anticlimactic position for the youth (present) and a climactic one for the aged (past). This is a testament to the assertion of change being the only permanent thing in life as life revolves and position changes. I think this is a strong message to all generations, regardless of location, belief system and culture.

My first encounter with the author of *Painted Butterfly: A Poetry Collection*, Mrs. Amaka Oguejiofo, was in the reading of her winning short story, "Just the Two of Us," entered for the Creative Minds Creative Writing Competition in 2018. The simplicity of her expressions and easy-to-relate-with descriptions of deep emotions, with the ability to be non-judgmental in the presentation of characters and their attributes were things that really fascinated me about her writing. It is, therefore not surprising that the same skills have been employed in the writing of the poems in this collection of poems. I hope that in the future the world will be intellectually provoked and engaged by many more poems from her stable.

Olubunmi A. Famuyiwa
Kwara State University,
Malete.
June 17, 2019.

PREFACE

Poetry is words performing acrobatics: Language that leaps, jumps, twirls, and spins arabesques. Poetry is words at their flying, swooping, tumbling best. It is prose in song; colourful arpeggios rendered in words.

I discovered a love for poetry in the two years or so since I joined Creative Minds on Facebook. You could say the genre snuck up on me and captured me. For me, poetry has become a medium to express emotions, to tease out from my inner man, pictures couched in words, and to arrange them in rhythmic order on white pages. It is an expression; and it is an oblation.

Painted Butterfly is my first collection of poetry. The subject matters are as eclectic as the multi-coloured wings of a butterfly. I have not paid absolute attention to rhymes and meter, but I have let my heart bleed with the ink unto these pages. Some of the poems are simple both in language and rendering, but I hope not naive. This book is my metamorphosis, my transformation from solely a prose writer to a dabbler in the rarefied field of poetry.

So I send this collection from my heart to yours with the hope that you will enjoy reading the poems as much as I enjoyed writing them.

Amaka Oguejiofo
Abuja, June 2019

Table of Contents

Foreword	*i*
Preface	*v*
Colours	*5*
Woman 1	*6*
Butterflies	*7*
Woman 2	*8*
Lost in the Crowd	*9*
Where Were You?	*10*
Prayer	*11*
Lost Loves	*12*
Falling	*13*
Of Forgetfulness	*15*
Amazon	*16*
Serenity	*17*
Inspiration	*18*
Day Break	*19*
Lost Loves 2	*20*
Happy Muse	*21*
How to Get a Man and Keep Him	*22*
Florida 1	*23*
Travelling While Black	*24*
Layers	*25*
Bouquet	*26*
Bird in a Guilded Cage	*27*
Locked in the Light	*28*
Wedding Day	*29*
Armistice Day	*30*
Step into My Heart	*32*

Just Because	33
Christmas	34
Lost Loves 3	35
Golden Synergy	36
Dream Weaver	37
Somewhere in the Sahara	38
Half the Picture	40
We are Salad	41
Jigsaw Puzzle	42
Me and You	44
Majesty	46
Dark Knights	48
Nature's Call	49
The Road to Libya	50
Catharsis	51
Break Up	52
Serenity 2	53
Heart Song	54
You Said	55
Evolution	56
Ask Me Why	57
Alzheimer's	58
Salute the Fading Sun	59
Full Moon Over the Sea	60
Time	61
Insight	62
Birth	63
Dawn	64

Waterfalls	65
Adam	66
We Were Like You	67
Song of the Beloved	68
Cry My Beloved Nation	69
Green Eyes	70
In Memory of a Promising Young Man	71
Change	72
Seasons	73
Vultures at Noon	74
Fallen Angel	75
Undercover	76
For Kadara Land under Siege	77
Finish	79
The Old Dyer	80
Blood on the Plateau	81
Easter	82
Hope	84
Bloody Roses	85
Girl Hawker at Night	86
Drumbeats	87
The Return	89
Corruption	90
The Vote Stealers	91
Political Dictators	92
Blossoming	93
Dancer	94

Borrowed Feelings	*95*
Woman 4	*96*
At the Ocean's Edge	*97*
Peace	*98*
Creativity	*99*
Nma Agha	*100*
Humanity	*101*
Flaming Passions	*102*
Scorpion	*103*
Evening Shadows Fall	*104*
Africa	*107*

COLOURS

Let me paint you a canvas of colours
Swiping and swirling in blues, greens and yellows

Let me make dainty brushstrokes in deep purple and
magenta, drawing you into a living canvas of hues

Let me paint you red, orange and ochre
Passions leaping and spanning the canvas

Let me ground you in greens and browns
Tying you to the earth and to me

Let me paint you a Masterpiece
In many colours; but I need to know
Will you be my muse?

WOMAN 1

She is the strength of a nylon thread
Pull too tight, and it cuts deeply into the flesh

She is the power of the storm
Full of electricity, fury and freshness

She is the womb that conceives and
The arms that receive

She is the warm milk stained chest
Soft, nurturing and uncomplaining

The fingers that soothe
The cool palm on a hot forehead

The beating heart of the earth

The root

The source

BUTTERFLIES

Fluttering flowers genuflect over rough vessels of nectar.

Dancing and drawing juices
Brushing pollen on stamens, creating new life

Giving as their own special gift to us, the beauty of two painted wings

The soul of the garden in summer

WOMAN 2

That you can see through me doesn't change the fact that I am made of metal and steel

There's no way through me.
I am high impact resistant. Kiss me and fall

Face upturned to the rising sun, I rise out of watery captivity

Fiber light, but dense as a diamond;
Delicate as a spider's web but with that same incredible tensile strength

I am woman. Look again; can't you see?

I am free

LOST IN THE CROWD

There are times I forget my lines, though
I know I should be witty, say something meaty

Times, I'm battling to remember how to be pert,
struggling to bring it up a set

Those times when the company is elite,
and the atmosphere is lit

When I'm absolutely meant to be the life and soul; out
there shimmering and glittering like a hot coal

But

I'm just not feeling it, because my heart is crying out...

Does no one understand? That I am right now having
doubts about my eminence,
second guessing my prominence?

If I walked away from here
If I never raised another cheer

Would anyone see me go?
Does anyone care that I'm low?

WHERE WERE YOU?

Where were you when I needed a friend?
Where were you when my heart beat hard with fear?

Where were you when I stretched out my hand, longing desperately for a human touch?
Where were you when tossing and turning I lay sick on my couch?

Well, I dialed your number and I heard:

"The person you are calling cannot be reached..."

I guess that's where you were. That's where you've always been.

PRAYER

Head bowed, heart lifted
Hush my soul.
Be quiet within me.
Let hope rise,
Let doubt fall
Look not at the trouble
But see the solution

Now, read the prescription
for peace -

In everything
By prayer and request
With gladness
Ask for your needs from Him
And serenity will shield your heart
Unto eternity

Now rest,
It is done

LOST LOVES

Are you the man in the moon?
Because stretch as I might I can't reach you
Must you be gone again so soon?
What exactly do you want me to do?

Sitting right here by you
Watching you lost in your phone
Makes me feel very alone
Aching and wondering what else to do

What can I ever do to be enough?
Sometimes you say I am too tough
Will it help if I cry and act clingy?
Won't that just make you feel guilty?

Are you the man in the moon?
Please love, just say you'll come back soon

I promise I won't move an inch
I'll be sitting here waiting for you

FALLING

Fallen into a deep well head first
I am lost in the dark waters of your love
Drowning in arbitrary emotions
Holding unto futile suppositions

I wish I had eyes-wide walked into this, or at least,
stopped at the brink and given it a thought

But I let myself go, and

I've tumbled into water too deep to swim
I've stumbled, fallen into liquid darkness both fearful
and dim

I'm gasping, out of breath,
Drowning in your stealth

Tears running down my face I ask,

Are you my lover, Sweets, or
am I your prisoner?

OF FORGETFULNESS

I cannot tell all I know
for Wisdom must keep a secret
She needs must pick this up and throw
it; dark, hidden thing that it is, into a deep pit

Listen to the song of the wind,
to its whispers and its sighs
Hear it comb the trees and sing
Of deep things out of mind

Songs of forgetfulness

For yesterday's sorrow
must not be allowed to kill the joys of tomorrow

I insist on that;

So I hand it all over to forgetfulness…

AMAZON

I buzz like a hornet and I sting like a bee
The midnight wasp has nothing on me
My strength is in endurance, and
like a puma I will pounce

Wreaking fear in the heart of the proud
Making hearts fail at my sound

Don't be deceived by my beauty
I am strong and I am doughty
Pinning my prey by force
Rising my hair to toss

I am the soul of war
The very heart of the storm
The breasted nightmare
In the field of battle

I am Amazon

SERENITY

Dimpled currents catch the rays of the sun
Dancing, serenading my peace
Waters splash and gurgle from fountains
Trapping rainbows in their spinning arms

So much beauty

Knocking at my heart's door
Peace opens the door to its embrace
Perfect accord

Here I build a temple to serenity

INSPIRATION

Stillness grows in me
Silence too deep for words
In this quiet my spirit hushes
My thoughts that are stored
In the serenity of introspection
Marinating, reaching fruition
Flow together
In blondes and rich ochres
Into a potent palette of colours
Painting a wide canvas with
dots and smears of Inspiration

DAY BREAK

The day wakes up, breathing out clouds of white on blue

Stretching elegant arms above the golden sun

Smiling in drops of joy on rolling green fields

Waking hearts both sad and eager to run the race again.

LOST LOVES II

Spent petals in deepest red
litter the floor of my heart

Echoes of a love that lived not but died
Forlorn and sad, here we part

For love does not live here anymore;
please shut that door

HAPPY MUSE

Who says it is not poetic to be happy?
Is the muse only for the darkness and gloom of loss?

Of failed loves and lost hopes?
Is it not also in the brightness of blue skies and floating clouds?

Of warm family hugs and comforting evenings on verandas open to the cool evening breeze? Slices of chilled watermelon anyone?

Is a baby's first tottering steps not a muse?
His happy giggles at finding he can stand?
Is baking my first ever cake not a worthy subject?
What of swimming in the glittering sea?
Is the happy sounds of children playing chase not enough grounds for a new poem?

Today, Muse be happy

HOW TO GET A MAN AND KEEP HIM

Be a little clingy, but not too clingy
Be a little needy, but avoid being too needy
Hide your strength under a tear
Sometimes you even pretend to fear
Because a strong and intelligent woman
remains a serious threat to a strong and intelligent man

FLORIDA I

White light stroking rippling waves with ghostly fingers

Waters breathing and cooling from the warmth of the day, bedding down for the night

Sighing and murmuring
Murmuring and sighing
Tossing and turning

Held in the sweet embrace of a warm Florida night

TRAVELLING WHILE BLACK

I've been tossed and harassed
Profiled and stereotyped
I've come under suspicion
With no circumspection
Been eyed and dyed
Scrutinized and intimidated
But my core is untouched
Solid and enduring as the ancient rocks

I am not who they think I am

I am me, no apologies

LAYERS

It is not for shame that an onion covers itself in layers

Each layer is a pungent affirmation of worth...

Scrape one off and there is another.
Cut through a section, and there are still more rings of value

The beauty of the onion is its rings

In the same way, the allure of a woman is in her layers

Each layer giving way to another layer in concentric mystery

BOUQUET

Here's a rose. It is red like the blood of my battles.
Here's a daffodil. It's amber glory speaks of my victory.

Here's some lavender. Majestic lilac hues announce my royalty.

Here's a daisy. Pure white petals speak about the indescribable peace that dwells within me.

Here's a bouquet of my life in all its colours and perfumes. Take it, hold it, smell it. It's beautiful; and it's all I have to give.

BIRD IN A GUILDED CAGE

Beyond lies freedom
Or is that what it is, really?

Yes,
There is open space out there
But it's ordinary as can be
Just a cold room with a window
And those trees out there
Is that the blue sky?
The sun shining in golden radiance?
Is that freedom?
Or is freedom this golden cage
With its silver lock and key?

LOCKED IN THE LIGHT

Cocooned in my womb of white waters
I am terrified
I fear your holding unto me, can't breathe
But I am even more terrified of your letting go

Certain death…

So this is my amphibious reality
I'm locked in the light
Breathing fear and death
Waiting for you to make up your mind
Breathless death or drop from a height?

Whatever you do
I'm begging you
Please please don't let me go

WEDDING DAY

At the first cock crow, meet me at the udala tree
Do not bring mpa n'aka. Let us meet by the light of the dying moon

That passion in your eyes, my love, let me see
Let that be my assurance that you will be mine, soon.

Come with your jigida dancing to the rhythm of your steps
Your firm shoulders balancing your head like a pretty gourd
Come to me as the day begins to prep
Come and whisper to me, "You are my lord."

Let me hold your hand in the dawning light
Let me embrace you in the secret cleft of the tree
Ngwugwu aga to ato ana tu ya mbo?

So listen, my love, I hear your mother's voice
Run to her quickly. Yes, do not delay, go!
My fingertips must yet part from yours, but tonight, yes tonight, you are mine.

ARMISTICE DAY

The warm lifeblood of millions soaks the soils of battle

Skulls stacked in pyramids of the slain

Ghostly battlefields echoing with the cry of the wounded

Trenches and trench foot in noisome holes in the ground

Boys barely grown clutching rifles in frozen fingers, dreaming of a mother's embrace

Tanks tearing across pitted fields

Mortars and fiery bullets flying like angry hornets

Battalions and brigades falling like ripe fruits from trees

They call it war
I call it the game of human ninepins
As long as men are men, there will be war.

STEP INTO MY HEART

Go ahead open the door
Yes, it creaks a bit doesn't it?
Push aside that web.
Go on, wipe the dust.
Light a fire and put on some tea.
Welcome back home.
It's good to have you back.

JUST BECAUSE

I loved you just because...
Your deep calling to my deep
Your dimples blinking your delight
Eyes sparkling like starlight
But they were not the whole story

What we had was way deeper
With you I touched bedrock as with no one before
You did not speak to my ears, you spoke to my mind

Subliminal connections

CHRISTMAS

In the still of the night
With darkness at its height
A glory burst forth, spanning the sky
It spoke of the fact that a Saviour was nigh

The skies above broke out in song
Angels spanning heaven and earth
For him mankind had waited this long
Now at his coming burst out great mirth

The bells are pealing
The nations are singing
Hope is springing
Heaven is smiling

For unto us a King is born

LOST LOVES III

Losing you was an amputation
I pine for your smell
Like sunshine on a summer garden
I long for your shade
Like the shadow of a slender rock

I'm sorry I cut us apart
Honey, I'm bleeding
Please come back

GOLDEN SYNERGY

My flames withheld from burning power
Douse themselves in the cool waters of night
My strength withheld from crushing force
Strokes the deep with fingers of gold

I am not weak, so please don't misunderstand me
The word you probably want is meek

Because, I am

A thousand detonations of energy
Hidden within a golden synergy

I am more than life force, I am Life.

DREAM WEAVER

I dream of you when I am awake
And see you in my sleep
Your presence is like a passing wraith;
I touch you and try to keep
You with me until I wake

Your love is like a wide cold lake
Deep enough to drown in
A parching thirst I cannot slake
A burning hunger deep within

Like ice to a fever
Like coins to a giver
You touch my soul and I quiver
I need no one to deliver

When ages end, for you I will still hunger
For You and You alone are my definer

SOMEWHERE IN THE SAHARA

It wasn't a failure of negotiations
There were none
It wasn't a true-to-life dramatization
This was real life; it was done

I saw it; I was there, I saw the
Piercing bullets flying
Terror rising
Panic overtaking
Men falling

Khaki, old and pale-washed by the desert sun, soaked in dark red blood
Eyes open to the pale blue sky, unseeing, staring at the failed national bond

While behind closed doors, vultures brood
Agents of death wrapped in a dark hood

Hands hovering over a chessboard
Whose pieces are pawns alone
Pushing tokens forward
To a fate that will create more dried bone

Out there...

Somewhere in the Sahara

HALF THE PICTURE

Half is what you get
The rest is a mystery
A smile is what you met
The rest is history

The ethos of the female
The mystique of She
Is the hidden that makes you scale
Mountains and rivers to see

As the coconut wraps itself within a husk inside a shell
protecting the waters and the meat

So is she

You must work to see below the surface
To the soul that she is...

WE ARE SALAD
(Nigeria at 58)

We are the crisp green of fresh lettuce hearts mixed in with salty egg whites and golden yolks

Joined to cool cucumbers and earthy carrots...

We are the crunch of crushed almonds tossed in olive oil with slices of meaty avocado

We are flashes of hot red tomato, side by side with innocent white cabbage slices in sweet combo with pungent onion and round green peas

None of us is salad all alone. You layer us, toss us all together, mix us up, and then, we become.

JIGSAW PUZZLE

Sad and broken
Pieces falling everywhere
Cracked in a pattern
That's filling me with fear

Will this piece of me ever fit with that piece of me ever again?

Jigsaw puzzle
Shot me through a nozzle
All smashed up and falling to pieces
Should have seen the indices

I hold the pieces of me in trembling hands
Brutal dye to my eye
I weep over the fading cracks
That say here forever you'll stand

And I wish I could take off this mask

I try, but I find the mask is me

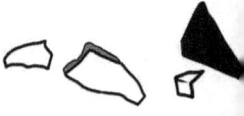

ME AND YOU

First, there was me, then there was you

We both grew from the soil through burning sands

We were surrounded by cool blue and shadowed by burning yellow

You grew for you and I grew for me

Somewhere in the middle, you touched me and I touched you

We danced around a bit, waving in the sublimely clear air

Then bit by bit we wound our arms around each other

You leaned on me, and I leaned on you

MAJESTY

I ride a stallion through quiet streets that have never acknowledged my inner queenship

In this land where I have worked my fingers to the bone, where I've been sneered at and treated like second hand goods

In this place where I have had my dignity impugned, where I have been called names like immigrant and minority

In the streets of my struggle;
I ride. My tears have dried long ago; I cry no more

I ride with measured stride, controlling the strength of my mount, making it obey me and yield to me as I have forced situations that broke others to yield to me

I ride, under a regal purple canopy turning my face with queenly elegance to view this city that has never known me

Tomorrow, I will walk again, but today, I ride
Today, they are permitted to see my inner majesty

DARK KNIGHTS

Echoes of truth
Resound in my soul, though
The bells still ring
Dark birds explode from the towers
Mocking birds settle and preen on the turrets
Calling out the arrival of strange minds
Cowled heads bowed in silent worship
Hands folded in loose sleeves
Slow in ghostly procession
Through bitter cold streets
Where pity has died
Love has been laid out on its back and
Charity gasps her last

NATURE'S CALL

I am the wind in the tree tops
I am the peacock's fanned tail
The gentle dew of morning
The painted sky at dusk
I am the chortle of running waters
The rainbow trapped in the waterfall
I am the rolling Savannah
The icy arctic
The downy newborn ostrich
The howl of the wolf at night
The giggle of the hyena
I hide in the crashing waves of the seashore
I brood in the gathering storm
I unleash in the lightning's stroke
Sleep with the waning sun
And when morning comes, I am renewed

THE ROAD TO LIBYA

Desert heat lays hold of supple flesh with dry, hooked hands

The hold of death and sudden destruction meted by roving bands of death merchants

The sandy way with its solitary lanes
unmarked by any hand of man

Uncharted wastes full of ancient mysteries

The dry lands sneer with disdain at feeble flesh and blood, turning them to desiccated mummies

Time and Man wait with the patience of twin vultures for others

to enslave

to destroy

CATHARSIS

My emotions, my passions
Explode with volcanic confusion
A wash of red lava flowing
From my inner core, fiery, glowing

Snaking down the slope of my heart
Threatening a conflagration
Of Titanic dimensions
Burning, razing, incinerating

Reaching out to destroy your pretensions
To make smoldering ashes your deceptions
Consume your contradictions
And calm my inner inflammations

BREAKUP

When I walk away
Don't beg me to stay
I've hurt in several places and made do
Wet my pillow through damp nights too
You've called me names
And caused me pains
Made me look small
Caused my life to stall
But I'm rising to my feet
I'm tired of being in a pit
It's turning around in my heart, coming together in my head
I'm not that person you say
I can strut, go out there and slay
So keep looking at me
And pretty soon you'll see

Me

And I'll be
Sashaying and shimmering
Straight out that door

SERENITY 2

It flows with the sweetness of melted chocolate
From the crown of my head to the soles of my feet
Wrapping me in its warm embrace
Soft and silky sweet
So rich and deeply satisfying

This peace within me
This Rest I've found

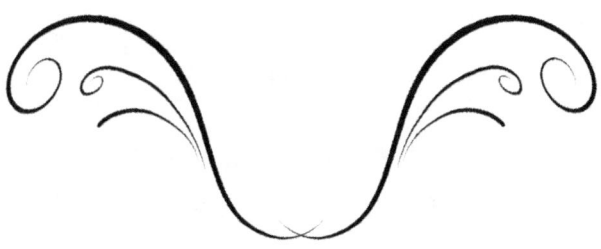

HEART SONG

Hold me like mist in your hands
Let me drift around you like wafts of perfume,
weave mysteries, spin lights

Call me what you want, and I'll be that;
But when the night comes, you must let me go

YOU SAID...

I was the gentle rain of June
The breeze that cooled you at noon
I was your secret desire
And your deepest passion
Your sun at high noon
Your moon in the darkest night
I was something new and something blue
Your earnest yearning
Your deep desire
That I kept you pining
Tossing and whining
You couldn't do without me
You just wouldn't let me be

So you took me to the altar
But since then, I've seen you falter
Passion falling like grey flakes
Burnt out of fires you made
Falling down down to the ground
Falling without a single sound

Now you tell me about irreconcilable differences
You say we're at different frequencies

Is that what kills love then?
The two words "I do" and a stroke of the pen?

EVOLUTION

Please be patient with me while I try to sort myself out
I'd like you to be still and listen to my heartbeat
Try to understand that I know, just like you do, that I don't have it all together
And the noise you hear is parts of me coming together
I'm becoming whole right before your eyes
Please be patient with me while I sort myself out

Please wait a little while, listen and you will hear some noises in the silence
That is God picking up the broken pieces of me and welding them together
If you feel some heat around me, it is ok to move back awhile
I'll be cooler by and by when the heat has settled
Can you hear some God noises in this silence?

Please be patient with me until it's all sorted out
Let potential and creative heat meet and meld
Watch me melt and gel and form again
From my knees, I rise to my feet, arms upraised
I am all formed now. He made me a Statue of Peace

ASK ME WHY

When you have walked a mile in my shoes, ask me why

When you have come so close and fallen short, be sure to ask me why

When assurance suddenly turns to doubt, ask me why

When light becomes darkness, remember to ask me why

I will be sure to answer, then, when you have lived my life and walked my path

And what other answer can there be?

It will be my turn to turn around and ask you why

ALZHEIMERS

The scent of days gone by clings to your clothing

In my mind you are sepia tinted, elegantly brushed and groomed

You tease the present with ghostly touches
That raise dust long since settled in my mind

I feel your hand on mine, and I look down at wrinkled skin and knotted veins

At age spots sprinkled like freckles on a sun kissed face

Where did the years go my love?
When did you leave me beloved?

SALUTE TO THE FADING SUN

As the golden sun pulls down its veil
And shadows stretch their dark arms
As the cool mystery of darkness wades in
And the tides go out
I stand unafraid
Here on the heights of life I stand
Gazing at its translucent waning
Glorious in my own beauty
Utterly fixed in my resolve

Unafraid of the dark, I salute the fading sun

FULL MOON OVER THE SEA

Wash the water with your waning rays
Peek from a cloud, keep darkness at bay
Paint my world in purples and deep reds
Prolong that last gasp, please do, I pray

But however long it takes, I must come to say...

It is enough, ruler of the spreading skies,
Sink out of sight, your debt is paid

TIME

The clock ticks,
time passes, and
things happen;
Lives lighten
Others darken
Hope rises
Despair deepens
Some strut
Some stagger
Progress dawns, yet
Death cheapens
the value of human living
for some others
But through it all
Wisdom will still call:
"Leave time
Forget chance,
Cease to mime
Another's life choices
For the best they have,
is still far less
Than what's ahead;
Do not starve your own
Muses

INSIGHT

Spanned by skirts of light
I spin among cosmic bights
Drenched in a snowstorm of stars
I dredge up memories of the scars
that form part of the geography
of the philosophy
of humanity,

I sit at the centre of the universe;

I am Insight

BIRTH

Inside the smooth oval
Domed and coloured like opal
Downy feathers curl
Tiny eyes close in deep lull
Life forces are pent up
In this, the lead up
to the crack
and sack
of gloom
and doom
Breaking forth into the light of day
New life comes into play
So, what do you think this is all about?
Well, dear friends, it's nothing too profound,
that's how chickens get to run around

DAWN

Cobbled clouds in pastel reds and deep purples smear the sky

The sun, a golden disc veined in red, rises from his bed of night,

shakes his golden tresses, and yawns across the heavens...

Life pours out of his light, gilding the earth

And out of the womb of time, a new day is born

WATERFALLS

Rainbow of waters cascading down;
we stand in wide-eyed awe at the force and colour of
nature unchained and running free

This spectacle of light, this stunning display, beckons
our hearts to bow in worship of the celestial Mastermind

We view this interplay of darkness and light, we scan
this tumbling pouring force of pure energy; we stand
overwhelmed with awe at this primal display of power

And we breathe just one word: "Amazed..."

ADAM

Rings of colour and texture,
Pulsing, radiant colour,
Verdure vibrant and green, stretch
far out and still further;
Peacocks preen, tails fanned in search of amour
Magnificent acres form the core
Of my delight
I breathe
Pure air
and scan horizons
emblazoned with beauty;
This is Eden,
I am back at the beginning…

WE WERE LIKE YOU

We were like you
We loved, we yearned, we loved and we lost

We were like you
We quarreled, we made up, we were misunderstood and we misunderstood someone else

We were like you
We fought, we made up, we tore the brokered peace to shreds and we fought again

We were like you
We learned, we wrote treatises, we philosophized and we made great discoveries

We were like you
We married, we procreated, we multiplied and we stretched out

We were like you
We travelled, we partied, we drank and we danced some more

We were like you
We lived, and then we died

SONG OF THE BELOVED

You give me light and the noise of cascading waters

I see myself glide from a dark place into your luminous light

You fill my life full of fresh greenness, until I am like a well-watered plain sprinkled with drops of dew

Always, with you, I know that my descent into the valley is nothing but my ascent unto the mountain top

So my heart lifts up, as I scan this beauty, and I realize beyond doubt that I am beloved.

CRY MY BELOVED NATION

I do not lament a country

No

That would imply a death, and to so imply, I cannot.
A thing has to have lived before you can say it died

Stillborn rather
Like an infant gone before it arrived

I speak of promise unfulfilled, potentials negatived.
A place dissolving into the red dust from which it
came; melting into a mud hole in the trackless rain
forest

Immolation not annihilation
Implosion not explosion

I do not lament a country, for one never lived

GREEN EYES

Strange how people hate
What they cannot mate
How envy attacks the heart,
Tackles it to the mat
And eyes fasten with malice
On the forbidden chalice
That is another's

If you get what I have,
Will it make you who I am?
Why do you find it difficult to love
Who you are? Why do you act a sham
of who I am?

I see you watch me across the room
And sister, your eyes are green
It's not even like I wiggle and preen
So why do you look at me with eyes of doom?

You can't be me
And you'll only be a poor copy if you try
So why don't you just go right ahead and be you?
And sister, set me free to be me.

IN MEMORY OF A PROMISING YOUNG MAN

It came like a hawk with metal talons
Diving in from a clear blue sky

It fell upon its prey like a bolt, scattering feathers in every direction
Striking with irresistible and irreversible force

Shattering hope, breaking resolve

Now all that's left is rivers of warm salt tears flowing down our puckered faces

Will this pain ever cease?

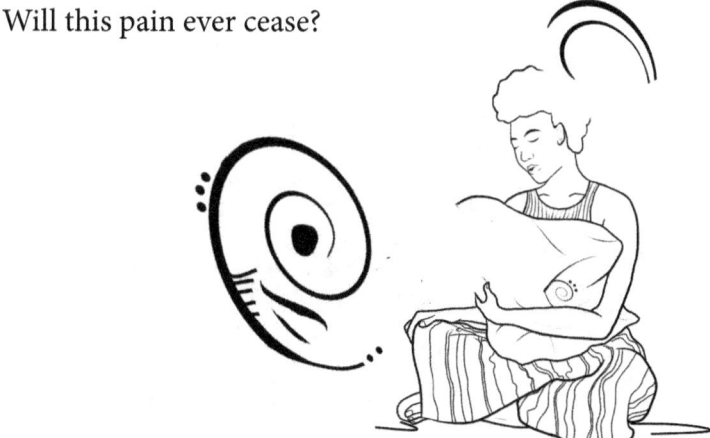

CHANGE

Different is not always better
Nor is change always the answer…

To jump from known to unknown
Can be a leap of faith
Or an invitation to disaster

By all means leap;
But before you do, look deep

SEASONS

Every tree has its season
Every life its reason
To run ahead of time is calamity
To hasten unduly, injury
You cry:
"But she has gone so far!"
"See him, he has become a star!"
But did you realize that success is relative?
And its cost prohibitive?
Just run in your own lane
And do not let hope wane
Remember, every tree has its season
And every life a definite reason

VULTURES AT NOON

While they yet screamed and danced at the victory, waving flags green, white and black

A dark horde jumped the divide between life and death and ushered an entire village into oblivion

Somewhere on a Rock called Aso, a vulture sits and broods

In the vaults of the earth, vats of human blood eddy and sigh

The eaters of souls and destinies rub their hands in glee

This is a game of power. Human beings are merely the chess pieces...

(In memory of the Jos dead)

FALLEN ANGEL

You fell with your spear in your hand
Why could you not take a noble stand?
You fell shining like the sun
Tumbling, turning, you were impaled on a thorn

You gave up your glorious liberty
For a sordid mess of vanity
You fell and doused your glory
Tumbling into a tank of stinking slurry

But even now bright angel,
You can free yourself and rise to mangle
Dark forces that would you entangle
Thrust deep with spear and break this shackle

Rise again and fly

UNDERCOVER

We see them pass,
and they look so assured
They hurry purposefully,
as if rock sure of their destiny
But it is what the eyes do not see
as we watch their confident progress
that unfortunately defines their very being;

Under that beautiful suit
is the fear of failure
the history of rejection
the little child whimpering in the dark
as "uncle" puts a familiar hand on their chest again,
the anxiety, as divorce looms closer
the feelings of inadequacy as the downsizing comes nearer

And so dear one, as you watch them pass,
their gait confident and bold,
envy no one, for each has a load you would be unwilling to carry,
if you only knew...

FOR KADARALAND UNDER SIEGE

Dark forms creep through the night
Entities of darkness hating the light
Armed with instruments of death left and right
Looking to strangle, slash and smite

Where go ye people of the dark lord?
For which mission do you waters ford?
Why the determination to cut the cord?
To raze, burn and bring discord?

We go to Kadara Land as bid
We run, we jump, we fly to kill
We do not falter, stumble or skid
We will not stop til we send them through the mill

We drink tears and blood; that is our food
We beat our chests, in pride we have stood
Instruments of destruction in our left hand and our right
We delight in our zeal; pride in our might

Now, hear ye dark hordes of the night
Cheetah or panthers though you be
Know for sure that He your powers shall blight

If you be warrior, King is He.

His roar causes the Savannah to tremble
With His stride no power on earth can meddle
He rises, he shakes his mane and advances
His puny foes He leaps and pulverises

Many days are for the destroyer
But one day, yes one day, is for the Redeemer

FINISH

Find it in you
Inside your healing heart
Not from a mind of iron or a will of steel
Intentions of amity and peace
Something that says enough
Hang the sword, end it

THE OLD DYER

The rich colours of the earth stain these fibers with their warm life

My old hands shake as they lift cords of cloth from the dyeing pit

This I have lived for all my life, embracing vibrant colours that will clothe the silky rich

The time has come

It is time to drop my tired arms and these skeins of colours

Who will pick them up when I am gone?
After I die, will anyone still dye?

BLOOD ON THE PLATEAU

They have defaced the rock on which proud nations stood

Altars to bloody gods form knobs on the great rock face

Gigantic tumors of death sprout from dignified crowns with missing heads.

Where are the Lords of the land? The ancient warriors?
Where are the owners of the land?
Asleep? Do they lie supine when death walks the land rattling its bones in its wake?

See a lava of molten red flow down the granite cliffs
We heard no eruption and yet the ground shook under the mortar fire of death

They sink, they lie, they die
Death jumps the barrier again and again
Falling they lie; lying, they die
The rock is covered with the blood of the slain
Flowing fiery red like lava from a volcano with no crater

Darkness falls across the land
There is blood on the Plateau

EASTER

In the cool, slightly damp darkness
A stirring

The rocks tremble
A great stillness

Power surges
In electric pulses

A stirring

And suddenly without warning
The Crucified dissolves through his grave clothes

Breaks totally free
From the chrysalis of death

He stands beside the cool slab of stone
For that one eternal moment, then
Slowly, deliberately, he unwinds the headpiece with pierced hands
Folds it gently and lays it where his head lay

With assurance
He approaches the boulder at the entrance
Touches it with the same superb confidence

And with triumphant step
He walks through the stone to endless life

It is Easter.

HOPE

The earth was dry and cracked.

Thirsty fissures cut through its bleeding heart. Wracked with drought, it burned beneath the blinding sun; not a drop of water fell from the sky above.

But out of this wasteland, as far as eyes could see, in a little corner tucked away amid the expanses of baked clay, a delicate green plumule pushed painfully through dry crust, unfurled and stretched its arms up to the burning sky, begging, pleading for rain upon the land.

BLOODY ROSES

Do pierced roses bleed?
Is their blood red,
Or does it flow black
Like deepest darkest midnight?

Do smiles fade?
Or do they journey to a place
Where brightness lingers
And sunshine has eternal yellow pincers?

Do hearts break?
Or are they held together
By cells you can't part asunder
By tissues you and I didn't make?

Does love die?
Does it burn to ashes
And yet leave behind a lie
That is nothing more than mere fantasies?

Must we part?
Or do we stay together
Like we have from the start
Of what is now a bother?

GIRL HAWKER AT NIGHT

Heaps of yellow mangoes
Jostle pyramids of guavas
Buy my wares
Buy my wares
I cannot go home until I have sold
At home my mother is old
She is beaten by life
Sundered by strife
Please buy my wares
Buy my wares
For you this is optional
For me it is foundational
You can walk away
But here I must stay
I cannot go home until I have sold
For at home my mother is old

DRUMBEATS

Raw skin stretched on sturdy sticks;
Dark fingers hammer out a rhythm
old as man
Agile legs kick and stomp
the heart of the brutal earth,
stamping out a beat as old as time
Is this joy?
Is this mourning?
It is none, and it is neithler,
It is the dance where death and life meet
and ages melt away in a furious rhythm
of feet and hands
Is this all?
Who will save Africa from the beat of the drums?

THE RETURN

Memories of hot black charcoal pots
Above glowing hearts of fire
The song dark skinned children sang
While roasting pears and corn
On cold rainy season nights
Swaying back and forth
Back and forth
Lulling tired eyes to sleep
Their music drowning the mating call
Of the night owl amock
It is a night to sleep
The sleep that is deeper than life
Peace dies in the darkness of this night

CORRUPTION

Sponsor of empty treasuries,
Corruption ushers in gangs that deal in usury,
Borrowing from nations to build a nation
Whose poverty belies its stupendous wealth
Its victims walk with legs like matchsticks past shops
selling breadsticks to those whose labour is theft of the commonwealth
Rolling past squalid stench pits in shiny metal coffins,
dealing out sour soup while they eat delectable muffins
Spreading abroad like strangler vines
Binding the nation with a dubious line
Building decorated skyscrapers
With a perforated exchequer
When the end comes,
We walk back into the darkness
Born from the loins of the chaos called corruption
Knowing that we never really began

THE VOTE STEALERS

Lines of humanity spiral to the ballot box.
We trudge to various centers in overgrown bushes, and also to the false palaces of sophistication in our crowded cities with no amenities
We brave bullets and threats from demagogues and warlords
to cast our votes
Hungry hours become bitter days of watching as center by center gives way to deadly theatrics
Ballot boxes grow legs and run into abandoned buildings
Private armies disappear with contestants
leaving behind photographs on ballot papers
Hope whimpers and dies
Courage abandons us and disappears
Meekly we watch the antics of the vote stealers
Patiently we listen to their announcements of victories at polls that never were...
Then we wait years to trudge again to centres in overgrown bushes and also to the false palaces of sophistication in our crowded cities with no amenities.

POLITICAL DICTATORS

Khaki and camouflage seemed to retire
Jackboots entered the closet and were hung
Barracks seemingly became sidelined
Their influence and power apparently suffered a hiccup
The tramp tramp tramp of marching feet
The shouted salute and the show of power
Weapons of death, bombs and bullets fleet
Declined into obscurity, hidden away in shelters
But under a dark cocoon of deception
Behold an incredible transformation
What was has come to be again
In a satanic exchange, an epic bargain
Sell us your future and your votes
For here we come again, sanitized, energized, transmogrified
In one hand your wealth stolen with military might
In another, death if you do despite
The throne of the nation, in consternation,
we timidly hand over to the self-same conflagration

BLOSSOMING

Suddenly,
A rippling explosion of brightness
A profusion of beauty
Little Krakatoas of eruptions
Blazing out in series
Clump by carmine clump bursting open
To reveal the heart of brightness

A living 4th of July

DANCER

Body twisting
Feet stomping
Waist gyrating
Hands and feet speaking
Eloquently
The pure language of rhythm
I can feel my energies peak
Forces consume me from within
Delicately
I pirouette
Stand still like a statuette
Tremble and kneel

I am eaten up; taken over

All I can do now is feel

BORROWED FEELINGS

Why should I borrow your sorrow?
Why must I cry as if there is no tomorrow?
Why can't you free me from this crushing weight of
expectations that never seem to abate?

I am one being, and you, another
So, let us live apart, though together

WOMAN 4

Fated to be a piece of chattel
Whether in peace time or in battle
When they talk about loot, and they hoot,
Whistling and grinning
It is me they mean
I am grist to their sin
I stroke their pride
Their references to me are snide
I am either an object or a project
Never a person
At any season
And for any reason

AT THE OCEAN'S EDGE

Rustling waves embrace the beach,
Wetting the edge of a continent and my naked feet
Warm waters shimmer into the distance
Speaking of horizons unknown
Their immensity seeming to dwarf my humanity;
Yet we sigh and roar in consonance

One heartbeat

Yearning, Waxing, Waning, Ebbing

Pulsating with primal life

The ocean is big,

I am bigger

PEACE

It is not the quietness of the graveyard
Where passions are forever stilled,
Nor is it the raging storm abated

Peace is not the shimmering waters of the sea catching the rays of the fading sun
Sounds of drops of water falling on a broad leaf one by one

Peace is not a baby's urgent wail quieted
when it is fed and sated on the breast

Peace, darling, is me sitting here with you
Hearts intertwined,
Conversing in silent whispers
Two lost in one

CREATIVITY

I was born in the cradle of silence
You bore down and pushed me out
Bloodily ashy, and yet full of credence

The quintessence of this process and its one true essence:

Stillness, quietness, deep silence

That is where my beauty was born

NMA AGHA

This shining length of metal
Edged in crimson blood
Token of warriors
Terror of foes
Obata otasu
Ngwo agha ndi odogwu
Is the force of life in my mouth
I speak, and something must die

HUMANITY

I crossed an ocean,
Only to learn
That man is man
Both here and there,
Whether indeed he is black or tan

FLAMING PASSIONS

Scattered and dazzling
Shining and overwhelming
Pulsating and glittering
My heart a thousand fires
Stoked by flames of desire
Heated like a furnace
Burning me to ashes, passions combining
With lust for your beauty

I realize;

You are not woman, you harpy,
You are famine

SCORPION

Poised, I skitter to the left, and then to the right
Armoured tail waving,
I strike to defend
I strike to oppress
I strike to survive

Do not blame me
After all,
Should they not fear one
Whose tail is laden with deadly poison?

EVENING SHADOWS FALL

The day is done
It is now sundown
Shadows creep
Deep regrets seep
Desire is dead, and
Only few debts are paid
Eternity stares, but there is
No time to repair
Offenses committed
Lies submitted as truth
The deep river calls
Life unfurls
The final journey begins...

AFRICA

Veins of yellow gold run through black rocks
The wealth of Mansa Musa in a single coffer
Skies of persistent blue fill up with grey clouds
Rivers snake their way through green earth tumescent with life
Scratch the soil, and an Iroko grows
Till it and barns overflow
Fecundity in adversity
The eternal paradox,
for mantling this black earth are the bones of the slain: rich fertilizer of blood and sweat
Filling the sunlit air are cries of the dying cut down by war, hunger and disease
Deep contradiction begging for an explanation
Battlefields where wealth and poverty fight and neither escape

www.ingramcontent.com/pod-product-compliance
Lightning Source LLC
Chambersburg PA
CBHW070433010526
44118CB00014B/2024